# THE BOSTON MARATHON
# **BOMBING**

# THE BOSTON MARATHON
# **BOMBING**

BY VALERIE BODDEN

**CONTENT CONSULTANT**
MORRIS TAYLOR
ASSOCIATE PROFESSOR, PUBLIC ADMINISTRATION
& POLICY ANALYSIS
SOUTHERN ILLINOIS UNIVERSITY

ABDO
Publishing Company

# CREDITS

Published by ABDO Publishing Company, PO Box 398166, Minneapolis, MN 55439. Copyright © 2014 by Abdo Consulting Group, Inc. International copyrights reserved in all countries. No part of this book may be reproduced in any form without written permission from the publisher. The Essential Library™ is a trademark and logo of ABDO Publishing Company.

Printed in the United States of America,
North Mankato, Minnesota
082013
112013

 THIS BOOK CONTAINS AT LEAST 10% RECYCLED MATERIALS.

Editor: Arnold Ringstad
Series Designer: Becky Daum

Photo credits: Justin Tang/The Canadian Press/AP Images, cover, 2; Marcio Jose Bastos Silva/Shutterstock Images, 6; Bizuayehu Tesfaye/AP Images, 10; Elise Amendola/AP Images, 13, 46; WBZ TV/AP Images, 15; John Tlumacki/The Boston Globe/AP Images, 16; Charles Krupa/AP Images, 19, 22, 92; Charles Dharapak/AP Images, 25; Julio Cortez/AP Images, 26; FBI/AP Images, 29; Melanie Stetson Freeman/The Christian Science Monitor/AP Images, 31; Rex Features/AP Images, 35; Massachusetts State Police/AP Images, 37; Spencer Platt/picture-alliance/dpa/AP Images, 38; AP Images, 41, 66; Steven Senne/AP Images, 43; Jose Luis Magana/AP Images, 48; The Lowell Sun & Robin Young/AP Images, 51; Rick Egan/The Salt Lake Tribune/AP Images, 55; Lisa Poole/AP Images, 58; Musa Sadulayev/AP Images, 63; Bob Leonard/AP Images, 69; Matt Rourke/AP Images, 72; M. Spencer Green/AP Images, 76; Robert F. Bukaty/AP Images, 81; ValeStock/Shutterstock Images, 83; J. Scott Applewhite/AP Images, 85; Dave Sandford/AP Images, 86; Sang Tan/AP Images, 88; Jim Young/AP Images, 95

Library of Congress Control Number: 2013941145

## Cataloging-in-Publication Data

Bodden, Valerie.
The Boston Marathon bombing / Valerie Bodden.
    p. cm. -- (Essential events)
ISBN 978-1-62403-054-3
Includes bibliographical references and index.
1. Boston Marathon bombing, 2013--Massachusetts--Boston--Juvenile literature. 2. Bombings--Massachusetts--Boston--Juvenile literature.  I. Title.
364--dc23

                                                            2013941145

# CONTENTS

# CHAPTER
# ONE

# FROM TRIUMPH TO TRAGEDY

The streets of Boston, Massachusetts, were quiet on the morning of April 15, 2013. It was Patriots' Day, a holiday in Massachusetts. The day marks the start of the Revolutionary War (1775–1783). The holiday means a day off work and school for many people. It is also the day on which the Boston Marathon is run every year.

By 6:00 a.m., runners had begun to emerge from their hotels into the chilly morning air and make their way to Boston Common, a large park in the center of the city. There they waited to board the school buses that would shuttle them to the race's starting line, 26.2 miles (42.2 km) away in the small town of Hopkinton. It seemed like the start of a perfect day.

To the Boston Marathon's organizers, the morning of April 15, 2013, looked ideal for the race.

# A Famous Marathon

Patriots' Day 2013 marked the one hundred and seventeenth running of the Boston Marathon. First run in 1897, the marathon is the oldest—and most famous—in the United States. Each year, it serves as the unofficial start to the US running season, even as it draws runners from around the world. For elite runners, winning the Boston Marathon represents the pinnacle of achievement. For amateurs, the glory is in just experiencing the run. For nearly all, the marathon is

## NEW ENGLAND'S PERFECT DAY

Celebrated both in Massachusetts and Maine, Patriots' Day is held on the third Monday of April each year. Speaking after the marathon explosions, President Barack Obama called the holiday "a day that celebrates the free and fiercely independent spirit that this great American city of Boston has reflected from the earliest days of our nation."[1]

The Boston Marathon is the highlight of Patriots' Day in Boston. The day is even sometimes called Marathon Monday. However, it is not the only special event held in honor of the holiday. For early risers, the day begins at 6:00 a.m. with a reenactment of the Revolutionary War battle at Lexington. Later, the Boston Red Sox baseball team plays a home game. The first pitch is thrown before lunch. That way, by the time the game is over, the fans pouring out of Fenway Park are just in time to join the crowds cheering for runners near the finish line of the marathon. The combination of all these special events once led writer Todd Balf to label Patriots' Day as "New England's Perfect Day."[2] Many in Boston agreed.

the reward for months of training, running through all types of weather at all hours of the day.

That training was necessary not only to run the race, but also to simply qualify for it. In order to register for the Boston Marathon, runners must complete another marathon within a specific time limit. Men ages 35 to 39, for example, must complete a marathon in 3 hours and 10 minutes, while women in the same age group must finish in 3 hours, 40 minutes.

## And They're Off

As those who would run the race got off the early morning buses in Hopkinton, they were ushered into the Athletes' Village. This large, grassy area dotted with huge tents served as a staging area as runners waited for their turn to start the race. Many runners spent their time talking, resting, stretching, or snacking in anticipation of the several hours of running ahead of them.

So many people run the Boston Marathon—23,000 people in 2013—that it is started in waves, or groups.[3] The elite women were set to start at 9:30, followed by the elite men at 10:00. The first wave of nonelite

The Athletes' Village gives runners a chance to rest, stretch, and socialize before they begin the grueling race.

runners would also start at 10:00, followed by another wave at 10:20 and a final wave at 10:40.

As the first runners approached the starting line, the sky was clear and sunny, and temperatures were still cool—just below 50 degrees Fahrenheit (10°C).[4] Crowds piled up along the sides of the street, many holding up homemade signs and screaming their support. At the sound of the starting gun, the runners took off. With nearly 8,000 runners grouped into each wave, it took almost ten minutes for everyone in a wave to cross the starting line. The crowd cheered the entire time. While the elite runners focused on setting their paces, many runners smiled and high-fived spectators as they ran past.

For the first mile, runners enjoyed a downhill run. By mile 2, they were out of Hopkinton and running through the town of Ashland, followed by Framingham, Natick, and Wellesley, the halfway point of the race. At mile 16, runners entered a stretch of seven hills that culminated at mile 21 with a 650-yard (590 m) climb known as Heartbreak Hill.[5] From there, runners ran through the town of Brookline before entering Boston at mile 24.5. Just a few more turns and they would be at the finish line.

## REMEMBERING NEWTOWN

The start of the 2013 Boston Marathon honored the victims of another tragedy. Before the starting gun sounded, 26 seconds of silence were observed for the 26 students and teachers who were killed in a December 2012 school shooting at Sandy Hook Elementary in Newtown, Connecticut. Among the spectators who had come out to watch the race were many from Newtown, who had no idea they would be witnesses to yet another tragedy.

## Spectator Sport

The Boston Marathon is famous for its runners, but it is also known for its spectators. Every year, half a million people line the 26.2 miles (42.2 km) of the racecourse to cheer the runners to the finish line. In 2013, children were there on family vacations to cheer on a mom or dad. College students were there to cheer on friends. Ordinary Bostonians were there to cheer on anyone and everyone. "The hardest thing about [running the Boston Marathon] is that the Bostonians want it just as bad as you do," said elite marathon runner Shalane Flanagan. "There were moments when I had chills, there were moments when my ears hurt they were yelling so loud."[6] The closer the runners got to the finish line, the thicker and louder the crowds got.

## To the Finish Line

The final half mile of the Boston Marathon takes runners down Boylston Street in the Back Bay neighborhood of Boston. By around noon, the elite men and women had

Lelisa Desisa crossed the finish line hours before tragedy struck the marathon.

reached the finish line. Lelisa Desisa of Ethiopia won the men's division with a time of 2 hours, 10 minutes, 22 seconds. The women's winner was Rita Jeptoo of Kenya, who ran the course in 2 hours, 26 minutes, 25 seconds.

The elite, however, represented only a small portion of the race's participants. Over the next several hours, runners continued to cross the finish line, many of them exhausted and near collapse. Once they crossed the line, volunteers greeted them and presented each one with a medal. The volunteers also provided much-needed water, food, and heat blankets.

By approximately 2:50 p.m., thousands of runners had crossed the finish line. Thousands more were getting close. Their friends and family members waited near the finish line, some even checking loved ones' progress with tracking apps. Their cheers were deafening. Reporters called the street "a tunnel of human noise."[8]

Among the spectators on Boylston at that time were Bill and Denise Richard and their three children. The family had gone to get ice cream and then returned to their spot near the finish line to watch for friends who were in the race. Krystle Campbell and her friend Karen Rand were also there. Both were cheering on Kevin McWatters, Karen's boyfriend. Lu Lingzi, a Boston University student from China, was watching the race with friends.

Jeff Bauman Jr. was at the marathon to watch his girlfriend cross the finish line. Brothers J. P. and Paul Norden were there to support a friend running the race. Eleven-year-old Aaron Hern watched for his mother, while 65-year-old John Odom was cheering for his daughter.

As these spectators and thousands of others continued to cheer, something went terribly wrong.

The blasts were captured in blurry television footage.

At 2:50 p.m., 4 hours, 9 minutes, and 43 seconds after the race began, a huge blast rang out near the finish line. Smoke filled the air, and people's cheers turned to screams. Ten seconds later there was another blast, approximately 100 yards (91 m) from the first.[9] The triumph of the finish line was forgotten. In its place was a tragedy.

# CHAPTER
# TWO

# RAPID RESPONSE

At first, many people did not know what was going on. Some thought the first blast was an ill-timed celebratory cannon or a blown electrical transformer. Others knew right away. With the second blast, nearly everyone realized what was happening: the marathon was under attack.

The force of the blasts knocked nearby people to the ground. Thick, sulfur-scented smoke covered the scene, and for many, everything sounded muted, as though they were hearing things from underwater—a result of the damage the bomb blasts did to their eardrums. Thousands of people ran away from the blasts in different directions, seeking a place where they would be safe from any further explosions.

## Heroes

Hundreds of others ran toward the blasts, seeking to help the injured. Among them were numerous police officers and emergency workers who had been stationed

Authorities worked quickly to clear the area after the bombs exploded.

at the race's finish line. Race volunteers, including doctors who staffed the medical tent, joined them, as did many runners and spectators. They raced to pull down the gates and fences placed at the sides of the road to keep spectators off the racecourse. On the other side of the fences, blood and broken glass covered the sidewalk. Bloodied and battered people lay moaning on the ground, many of them with missing or severely

## THE COWBOY HERO

Pictures of the explosions at the Boston Marathon hit Twitter and other social media sites within minutes of the blasts. One of the most widely circulated showed a victim with bloodied legs being wheeled from the scene by a man in a white cowboy hat. The victim was 27-year-old Jeff Bauman, and his rescuer was 52-year-old Carlos Arredondo. Arredondo was at the race to hand out American flags as a tribute to his sons, Alex, who was killed in Iraq in August 2004, and Brian, who had committed suicide in 2011.

Arredondo had been across the street from the blasts, but as soon as the bombs exploded,

he ran to help, jumping the fence to get to the opposite sidewalk. The first person he saw was Bauman, whose shirt was smoldering. Arredondo put out the flames with his hand, then turned to Bauman's legs. The lower parts of both legs were gone. Arredondo and another bystander used a T-shirt to make a tourniquet. Then he put Bauman in a wheelchair and ran him toward the medical tent. He stayed with Bauman until the injured man was loaded onto an ambulance. Both of Bauman's legs had to be amputated, but his family is grateful to Arredondo. "The man in the cowboy hat—he saved Jeff's life," said Bauman's stepmother.[1]

Carlos Arredondo, *center*, was among the ordinary citizens who aided victims in the aftermath of the attack.

mangled legs or feet. Some had terrible gashes or burned, blackened skin.

Police officers and other responders quickly did what they could to help the most seriously injured. Many used belts or shirts to tie tourniquets on victims' legs. Others covered people up to keep them from going into shock. Some picked up the wounded and ran with them toward the medical tent, where a triage clinic was quickly set up. Others made use of the wheelchairs left at the finish line for runners whose legs gave out or cramped up after the race.

Sirens began blaring at the explosion site less than two minutes after the first blast. Soon the sound became deafening as every ambulance in the city was dispatched to the finish line. Before being loaded onto ambulances, victims were rushed to the medical tent, where they were stabilized and categorized based on the severity of their injuries. The atmosphere in the tent was calm and organized as doctors worked on patients and then quickly sent them to ten area hospitals to avoid overwhelming any one facility.

## Prepared for Action

Within 20 minutes of the attacks, patients began to roll into the hospitals, sometimes two in one ambulance. Many were losing so much blood they were within minutes of death. Doctors worked feverishly to repair severed arteries and damaged blood vessels and close gaping wounds. In many cases, they had to decide whether to save or amputate legs because injuries were so extreme. Other patients needed shrapnel—in the form of BB pellets, nails, glass, or other debris—removed. Some patients had 40 or more pieces of this shrapnel embedded in their bodies, most of it in their legs and feet.

Many would need additional surgeries in the days ahead, but for now, the doctors' goal was simply to save lives. And they did. All of the patients brought to hospitals survived. In total, 264 people were injured in the explosions. At least 14 of them lost limbs.[2]

Three people died before they made it to a hospital. They were 8-year-old Martin Richard, 29-year-old Krystle Campbell, and 23-year-old Lu Lingzi.

Experts credited the high survival rate to many factors. Chief among them was the quick response of emergency personnel and bystanders on the scene. In addition, patients were quickly and efficiently transported to local hospitals. Emergency planning and drills at those hospitals meant they were ready to spring into action. Boston was also an ideal location for treating the wounded, since six hospitals specializing in

The quick, orderly action of medical workers contributed to the high survival rate, even among those with horrific injuries.

trauma were located within three miles (4.8 km) of the bombing.[3]

## Separated and Searching

As word spread about the explosions, people who had not been near the blast sites frantically tried to contact loved ones they knew had been near the finish line. Many people tried to reach one another over the phone, but cell service was overloaded, and most calls would not go through. Some people were able to send and receive text messages, and others turned to social media in the quest to reconnect. Many sent messages through Twitter or Facebook. Others used a person finder tool launched by Google. The searchable Web site helped people learn whether their loved ones had been accounted for.

People near the attacks used social media to post photos, videos, and personal accounts of the bombing almost instantly. Some of these firsthand views of the bombings were shared thousands of times as word of the attacks spread across the world.

## Securing the Scene

Once the injured had been cleared from the immediate vicinity of the blast, police officers and investigators worked to secure what was now a 12-block crime scene. As people fled from the blasts, many dropped everything—including backpacks and other bags. Police were now confronted with a daunting task: make sure none of these bags contained additional bombs. As the bomb squad and bomb-sniffing dogs searched the scene, rumors flew among the public and the media that unexploded devices had been found. The reports turned out to be false. Authorities eventually confirmed the two exploded bombs had been the only weapons on the scene.

Even so, officials could not be sure the threat of attack was over. They urged Boston-area residents to stay home. Flights were grounded for much of the day. Boston's police commissioner requested people not gather in large crowds.

## The President's Address

Just over three hours after the attacks, US president Barack Obama addressed the nation from the White House. He offered his thoughts and prayers to the people affected by the bombing. The president urged Americans not to "jump to conclusions before we have all the facts." But he promised, "We will find out who did this; we'll find out why they did this. Any responsible individuals, any responsible groups will feel

Shortly after the attacks, President Obama pledged the bombers would be caught.

the full weight of justice."[5] He had no way of knowing the responsible individuals would be identified only days later.

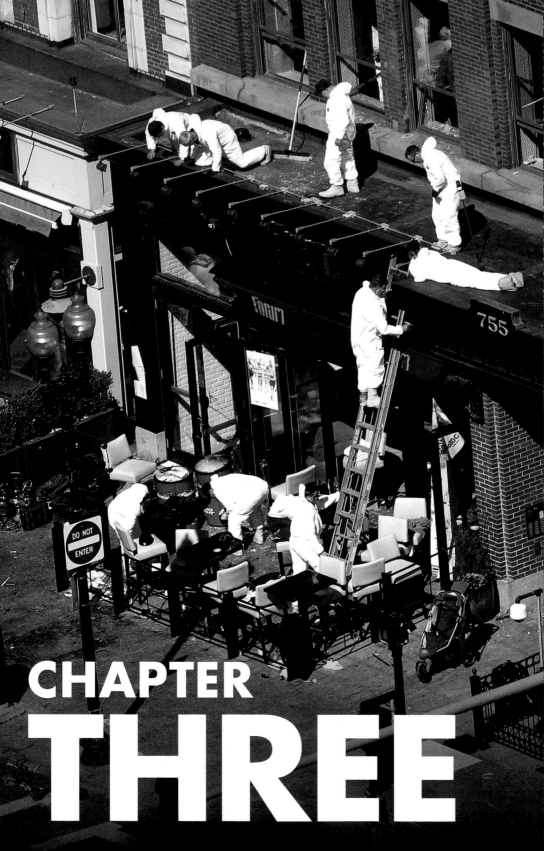

# CHAPTER
# THREE

# THE MANHUNT

Investigators did not lose a moment in attempting to figure out who had placed the bombs at the marathon. Facing the possibility of another attack, the Federal Bureau of Investigation's (FBI's) Boston Joint Terrorism Task Force mobilized for an investigation. The task force involved investigators from more than 30 agencies, including the FBI, the Boston Police, the Massachusetts State Police, Homeland Security, and the Bureau of Alcohol, Tobacco, and Firearms.

As soon as the crime scene was secured and investigators were certain there was no immediate threat, they began collecting evidence from the site. By Tuesday morning, investigators in special hazmat suits had begun to pick up remains from the blast. They recovered BBs, nails, pieces of black nylon that appeared to be from a backpack, and fragments of a pressure cooker. Everything was sent to a laboratory in Quantico, Virginia, for analysis.

Investigators quickly swarmed the area, including the roofs of nearby buildings.

Investigators also talked with witnesses, including Jeff Bauman Jr., a 27-year-old spectator who lost both legs in the blast. While still being treated for his injuries, Bauman told police a man in the crowd had caught his attention in the moments before the blast. The man was wearing heavy clothes and was not paying attention to the race. "He just didn't seem right. You know how you size somebody up? I just looked at him. I was like, 'what's this guy's problem?'"[1] Bauman described the man to a police sketch artist.

## Help from the Public

Even with these pieces of evidence, investigators were unable to identify a suspect. But they knew the marathon had been one of the most photographed events in the country on April 15. Thousands of spectators were snapping pictures or taking videos as their loved ones crossed the finish line. News crews were reporting from the site. Surveillance cameras from nearby stores and restaurants included views of the street. Investigators were eager to look at all of these images. They knew that somewhere in them was likely a picture of the suspect or suspects. The FBI called on anyone who was near the scene when the bombs exploded to send in their images.

Investigators discovered video footage of two men who walked together, carried backpacks, and showed little reaction to the explosions.

By Tuesday afternoon, they had received more than 2,000 tips, and more continued flowing in.[2]

Investigators then began the painstaking process of going through thousands of images and hours of video footage in an attempt to reconstruct the crime scene. They were aided by advanced software that could track unusual behavior and recognize faces. By Wednesday, April 17, investigators had discovered surveillance footage showing a man leaving a bag near the site of one of the explosions. After sifting through more images, investigators identified another suspect who appeared to have been walking alongside the first. Investigators did not know it yet, but the two men were Dzhokhar and Tamerlan Tsarnaev.

Although investigators now had the faces of their suspects, they had no names to go with them. On Thursday, they decided to release the images of the suspects to the public in the hope someone might be able to identify them. "For more than 100 years, the FBI has relied upon the public to be its eyes and ears. . . . We know the public will play a critical role in identifying and locating these individuals," said Richard DesLauriers, head of the Boston division of the FBI, at a press conference accompanying the release of the images.[3] DesLauriers also warned that the suspects were "armed and extremely dangerous. No one should approach them. No one should attempt to apprehend them except law enforcement."[4]

## Media Mistakes

On April 18, images of the suspects were posted to the Internet on the FBI's Web site, and they quickly made their way through social media. Many social media sites had already been busy trying to identify suspects on their own. On sites including Reddit and 4chan, users

Following the attacks, many online and television media outlets tried to deliver immediate information at the expense of accuracy.

had been examining photos and videos of the marathon, marking anyone they thought looked suspicious because they were alone or carrying a backpack. Many users began to accuse innocent people of the bombings based on the photos and videos they saw.

Social media sites were not the only ones to make mistakes. Many traditional media outlets picked up on and published rumors. On Wednesday, cable network CNN had reported an arrest had been made in the case, and other news outlets picked up the claim. The Boston Police Department took to Twitter to correct the misinformation. On Thursday, the *New York Post* printed a front-page picture of two young men at the marathon with backpacks; they turned out to have had nothing to do with the attack.

## Desperate to Escape

Investigators did not know it at the time, but in the days after the attacks, the suspects—later identified as 26-year-old Tamerlan Tsarnaev and his 19-year-old brother, Dzhokhar—had been hiding in the open. Only hours after the attack, Dzhokhar tweeted, "Ain't no love in the heart of the city, stay safe people."[5] The next day, Dzhokhar hung out with friends and worked out in the gym at the University of Massachusetts Dartmouth, where he was a student. Tamerlan, who was married and had a 3-year-old daughter, went home to Cambridge, just north of Boston. He went to the grocery store and took his daughter to the park.

The public release of their pictures as suspects on Thursday apparently shattered the Tsarnaevs' belief they could resume their old lives without detection. On Thursday night they began a desperate escape attempt. At 10:20 p.m., the brothers allegedly shot and killed Sean Collier, a 27-year-old police officer at the Massachusetts Institute of Technology (MIT) in an attempt to steal his gun.

After fleeing from MIT, the Tsarnaevs carjacked a Mercedes sport utility vehicle and told the driver they were responsible for the Boston Marathon bombings. Tamerlan drove the Mercedes while Dzhokhar followed in the brothers' green Honda Civic. After driving around for half an hour, the brothers stopped at a gas station in Cambridge, where the carjacking victim managed to escape and call police.

Police quickly located the stolen vehicle and began a six-mile (10 km) car chase.[6] As they fled from police,

## TRYING TO PROTECT A FRIEND

As investigators searched Dzhokhar's dorm room in the days after the bombing, they quickly discovered that three of his friends had removed evidence from it. When Dias Kadyrbayev and Azamat Tazhayakov, both from Kazakhstan, and American Robel Phillipos first saw a picture of the suspects in the manhunt, Kadyrbayev texted Dzhokhar that one of the pictures looked like him. Dzhokhar responded, "lol" and "you better not text me."[7] Dzhokhar also invited Kadyrbayev to take anything he wanted from his room.

Kadyrbayev, Tazhayakov, and Phillipos went to Dzhokhar's dorm room, where they found and took a backpack of fireworks with the powder removed, a jar of Vaseline, and Dzhokhar's laptop. Becoming more and more convinced that Dzhokhar had been involved in the bombing, they decided to protect him by throwing the backpack into a dumpster. Authorities later recovered the backpack from a landfill and retrieved the laptop from Tazhayakov. The two Kazakh students were charged with concealing evidence, which carried a possible $250,000 fine and five years in prison. Phillipos faced charges of lying to investigators, which could lead to a $250,000 fine and eight years in prison.

the brothers threw homemade bombs out the car window. By 1:00 a.m. on Friday, April 19, the chase stopped in the city of Watertown, where the brothers got out of their cars and engaged in a gunfight with police. According to neighbors, the brothers also continued to lob explosives at officers. During the battle, more than 200 rounds were fired, and officer Richard Donohue was shot and seriously injured.[8]

The firefight ended with the shooting of Tamerlan Tsarnaev. Dzhokhar jumped back into the stolen car and fled the scene, running over his older brother on the way. Tamerlan was transported to the hospital, where he was pronounced dead. On the way, the FBI scanned his fingerprints and finally learned his identity. Tamerlan's fingerprints were already on file with law enforcement because he had been investigated before.

## Lockdown

Meanwhile, Dzhokhar continued to elude authorities. Soon after speeding away from the gunfight, he abandoned the vehicle and continued his escape through Watertown on foot. As thousands of police officers descended on the area in full protective gear, they warned residents to stay inside. At 6:00 a.m., the entire

A resident of Watertown took photos of the brothers as they took cover behind the stolen car during the firefight.

Boston area was put under lockdown, with residents being told by the Boston Police Department to "shelter in place" and open their doors only to police officers.[9] Businesses remained closed, and roads were nearly empty. In Watertown, police began a house-to-house search in neighborhoods where they thought Dzhokhar might be hiding.

Residents not evacuated from their homes remained indoors, many of them peeking out windows and snapping pictures and videos of the police search that they shared through social media. Some also tuned in to local police scanners, live feeds of police radios available to the public, and then tweeted what they were hearing. On Friday morning, the Boston Police Department sent out its own tweet asking users to stop compromising officer safety by broadcasting their positions. Eventually, two online scanner Web sites went offline temporarily so police could conduct their investigation without fear the suspect might be alerted to their position. Millions of people around the country followed news of the search on television or online.

## Captured!

By 6:00 p.m. Friday, police had begun to wind down the search, which had so far found nothing. The lockdown for the Boston area was lifted, and residents tried to get back to life as usual. After a long day indoors, Watertown resident Dave Henneberry went outside to check on his boat around 7:00. As he pulled back the tarp covering the boat, he noticed blood inside. Then he saw a body. He ran from the boat and called 911. Within minutes, police were on the scene. A police helicopter used a heat sensor to monitor Dzhokhar's movements in the boat. On the ground, a robotic arm was used to lift the tarp in case

Heat-sensitive cameras showed a body in Henneberry's boat.

more explosives were in the boat. Believing the suspect was about to fire on them, police also engaged in further gunfire with the suspect, although some later reported that no gun was found in the boat. Police then tried to negotiate with the suspect, urging him to come out of the boat. Finally, around 8:30 p.m., a weak and bloody Dzhokhar was apprehended.

As thousands of police officers on the scene applauded, they were joined by neighbors who stepped outside to cheer for them. Neighbors continued to celebrate with parties and fireworks, and the Boston Police Department sent word around the world with a tweet: "CAPTURED!!! The hunt is over. The search is done. The terror is over. And justice has won. Suspect in custody."[11]

# CHAPTER
# FOUR

# SAYING GOOD-BYE

E ven as the country rejoiced in the capture of Dzhokhar Tsarnaev, the people of Boston continued to mourn for those who had been killed or injured in the attack. Before the drama of the chase took place, the first memorial service for the victims had already been held. On Thursday, April 18, President Obama offered words of encouragement at an interfaith service in Boston: "We may be momentarily knocked off our feet. But we'll pick ourselves up. We'll keep going. We will finish the race."[1]

With the manhunt behind them, the people of Boston—and all of Massachusetts—observed a moment of silence at 2:50 p.m. on Monday, April 22, to mark the one-week anniversary of the attacks. Afterward, church bells throughout the city and state tolled.

## Krystle Campbell: Always Smiling

That same day, the first funeral services were held for victims of the attack. The first to be buried was Krystle

The interfaith service on April 18 was held the day before the apprehension of Dzhokhar Tsarnaev.

39

Campbell, a 29-year-old restaurant manager who tried to go to the Boston Marathon every year. Immediately after the attack, Campbell's parents had been informed that their daughter had been seriously injured. But when they rushed to the hospital to see her, they discovered that it was Campbell's friend Karen Rand who had survived, not Campbell. "She was a wonderful person. She was sweet and kind and friendly and she was always smiling," her mother, Patty, said the day after the attack.[2] Everyone who knew her seemed to agree.

Campbell's funeral service was held at Saint Joseph's Church in Medford, Massachusetts, just north of Boston. More than 1,000 people filled the church to overflowing, with hundreds more left outside.[3] In addition to Campbell's family and friends, the funeral was attended by coworkers, political officials, police officers, and strangers who had never met her but wanted to pay tribute to those killed in the attack. Reflecting what so many had said about Campbell's personality, during the service the Reverend Chip Hines talked about Campbell as "a smiling, happy, youthful, selfless person," according to Annemarie Harvey, a friend of the Campbell family.[4]

Martin Richard, *left*, Krystle Campbell, *center*, and Lu Lingzi, *right*, were the three bystanders killed by the bombers.

## Lu Lingzi: Outgoing Student

On Monday night, more than 850 people gathered at Boston University for a memorial service to remember Lu Lingzi, a 23-year-old graduate student from China.[5] Among those at the service were Lu's parents, who flew to the United States in the aftermath of the attacks. Her father, Lu Jun, delivered a eulogy in honor of his daughter: "She set her life and career goals early, determined to go abroad and see the world. . . . Her compassion, sweet voice and beautiful smiles will stay forever in my heart."[6]

Lu had been near the end of her first year of graduate studies in statistics at Boston University, and in a letter to the school, her parents wrote, "While she was here, she fell in love with Boston and its people."[7] Classmates and professors remembered Lu as a dedicated student who was also friendly and outgoing. In the wake of the attack, Boston University established a scholarship in Lu's memory.

## Martin Richard: Active Eight-Year-Old

On Tuesday, April 23, eight-year-old Martin Richard was buried in a private funeral service for family. Throughout the week after the attack, members of the Richard family's neighborhood of Dorchester had left flowers and stuffed animals at the family's home. Many shared their memories of Martin with reporters. The picture they painted was of an active third grader who loved to play soccer, basketball, and baseball. "He had this grin, like he always had something funny he was thinking about," said family friend Christina Keefe.[8]

Even as they mourned for Martin, the Richards were also reeling from injuries sustained by other members of the family. Martin's younger sister, Jane, lost her left leg below the knee. In addition, his mother, Denise, lost sight in one eye, and his father, Bill, suffered shrapnel wounds, burns, and hearing loss. Martin's 11-year-old

A memorial to the victims was set up near the Boston Marathon's finish line.

brother, Henry, was also at the race but was not injured in the blast.

## Sean Collier: Dedicated Officer

MIT police officer Sean Collier was also honored in a funeral service on Tuesday, followed by a memorial at MIT on Wednesday. More than 10,000 people attended the service at MIT, including Vice President Joe Biden, Senator Elizabeth Warren, and thousands of police officers, some from as far away as Canada.[9] Collier's brother Rob Rogers said Collier would have loved the memorial: "People ask me, if Sean were here, what would he think? Are you kidding me? He would love this. You've got sirens, flashing lights, formations, people saluting, bagpipes, taps, the American flag. He would have loved it."[10]

The 27-year-old Collier was remembered as a dedicated police officer who took the time to make friends with many of the students on MIT's campus. "I believe he had the calling," said John Difava, MIT police chief. "He just wanted to be in law enforcement. It wasn't about the pay or the benefits or the retirement. It was about what law enforcement was supposed to be all about, that's to help people. He was a master at helping people."[11]

## Recovering from the Blast

By April 22, approximately 50 people injured in the marathon blasts remained in the hospital.[12] Many had already undergone multiple surgeries to work on amputated limbs, clean out shrapnel, set broken bones, and repair damaged veins and nerves. Many needed plastic surgery and skin grafts to close wounds. Some also fought off life-threatening infections.

Among those still recovering from their wounds were 33-year-old J. P. Norden and his 31-year-old brother, Paul. Each lost a portion of his right leg in the explosion in addition to suffering burns and shrapnel wounds. The brothers, who worked together as roofers, were taken to separate hospitals after the attack. Their mother, Liz, traveled back and forth between the two each day.

Multiple members of other families remained hospitalized as well. Celeste Corocoran lost both legs below the knee, and her 18-year-old daughter, Sydney, also suffered severe leg injuries. Newlyweds Patrick and Jessica Downes lost their left legs below the knee. Alvaro Galvis and his wife, Martha, both suffered severe shrapnel injuries, and Martha also lost a finger on her left hand.

## WHAT IFS

In the hours and days after the race, many of those close to the finish line began to consider what might have happened if they had gotten there a little sooner or a little later. Psychiatrist Brent Forester, who crossed the finish line minutes before the explosions, wrote, "And then the 'what ifs' race through your mind: What if I had taken my usual port-o-potty break or not pushed through those last few miles to break the four hour mark? I cannot really think about these realities."[13]

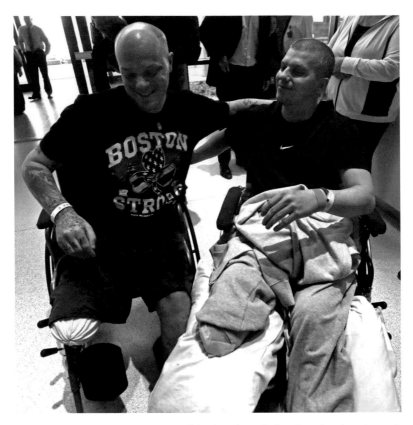

Victims of the bombing helped each other through the rehabilitation and recovery processes.

## Moving Forward

Even while burying the dead and comforting the wounded, the people of Boston began to move forward with their lives. Many remarked on how calmly the city and its people had responded to the attack. Peter Canellos, an editor at the *Boston Globe*, noted that people responded much more calmly to the marathon bombing than they had a decade earlier to the 9/11 attacks. "I would have expected more of a 'My God, it couldn't happen here' reaction. But people have been aware now for more than 10 years that it could happen here. They were sort of mentally prepared for it," he said.[14] On Wednesday, April 24, the area around the finish line on Boylston Street was reopened to the public, although police continued to stand guard in the area.

## MOVE ON OR MOURN?

In the days after the attack, the people of Boston tried to move forward. Commentators disagreed about the best way to do so. Writing in the *New York Times*, columnist Thomas L. Friedman urged the people of Boston: "Let's repair the sidewalk immediately, fix the windows, fill the holes and leave no trace—no shrines, no flowers, no statues, no plaques. . . . Let's defy the terrorists, by not allowing them to leave even the smallest scar on our streets."[15] Instead of a memorial at the site of the blast, he urged donations be made to charities in the victims' names. Friedman further asked Americans not to allow the attack to make them fearful or drive them into hiding.

Other commentators criticized Friedman's response. In an article published in the *New Republic*, Leon Wieseltier wrote that fear was a natural response to terrorism. "Americans were terrorized, on the day of the bombing and on the day of the manhunt; and they were right to be terrorized, because what they had in their midst was terrorism." He accused those who were eager to move on of underreacting to the event. "Mourning, and the time it takes, is not a victory for the terrorists. . . . There is a scar," he said.[16]

# CHAPTER
# FIVE

# THE TSARNAEV BROTHERS

With Dzhokhar Tsarnaev in custody, officials now knew who had carried out the attacks, but they still did not know why. They knew the brothers were ethnic Chechens who had spent parts of their childhood in Kyrgyzstan, Chechnya, and Dagestan. These areas once belonged to the Soviet Union. Kyrgyzstan is now an independent nation, though Chechnya and Dagestan remain parts of Russia. But the brothers had lived in the United States for more than ten years. Dzhokhar had become a US citizen, and Tamerlan was a permanent legal resident. "Why did young men who grew up and studied here, as part of our communities and our country, resort to such violence?" President Obama asked in a televised address after Dzhokhar's capture.[1]

To learn why, investigators would have to dig even deeper. Hundreds of FBI agents and police detectives

Federal agents soon began interviewing the friends and family of the brothers to learn more about them.

remained on the case, trying to piece together information about the Tsarnaevs' past, their motives, and any possible connections to terrorist organizations. In their search for answers, investigators interviewed friends and associates of the brothers, including other ethnic Chechens living in the United States. Some investigators even traveled to Russia to learn more about the brothers and interview their parents, who had moved back to Dagestan. Other investigators searched the brothers' homes, phone records, and computers as they began to piece together information on the brothers' lives.

## Seeking Asylum

Tamerlan and Dzhokhar Tsarnaev came from a troubled part of the world. Tamerlan was born in 1986 in the Russian territory of Kalmykia near the

Tamerlan, *left*, and Dzhokhar, *right*, lived in war-torn regions of the world as children.

Caspian Sea. Soon afterward, his parents moved to Kyrgyzstan, where the family expanded with the birth of two daughters. In 1993, Dzhokhar was born. The Tsarnaev family moved briefly to Chechnya but fled back to Kyrgyzstan when Russia invaded in 1994 to prevent Chechen independence. Around 1999, the family left Kyrgyzstan when ethnic Chechens faced persecution. The family moved to Dagestan before deciding to seek a new life in the United States.

Dzhokhar and his father, Anzor, came to the United States in April 2002. Anzor sought political asylum for himself and his nine-year-old son based on the persecution they had faced in Kyrgyzstan. The rest of the family, including 16-year-old Tamerlan, arrived in approximately 2003. The family moved into an apartment in the Boston suburb of Cambridge. Anzor, who had worked in a legal office in Kyrgyzstan, repaired cars on the street for ten dollars an hour. The family continued to practice Islam, as they had before moving to the United States, but they rarely attended a mosque or even talked about religion.

## UNEXPECTED SUSPECT

When they learned Dzhokhar was one of the suspects in the marathon bombings, his friends and former teachers and classmates were in disbelief. "I have had almost two weeks to think about it, and it still makes no more sense than the day I found out it was him. Nothing seemed out of the ordinary," said Jason Rowe, Dzhokhar's former college roommate, after the attack.[3]

## Fitting In

Although Dzhokhar knew little English when he first arrived in the United States, he quickly picked up the language and found it easy to fit into his new culture. In 2007, he entered Cambridge Rindge and Latin School, a public high school in Cambridge. He became a dedicated student and a star wrestler. Dzhokhar easily made friends at the diverse school, which included both immigrant and American-born students. Various friends described Dzhokhar as a "cool guy," a "great student," and a kid with a "heart of gold."[4] "He was just this scrawny little kid who was always giggling and happy. I can't remember him saying a mean word in his life," said Juliette Terry, a friend who had known Dzhokhar since elementary school.[5] Teachers and friends saw him as a "normal American kid."[6]

## THE TSARNAEVS AND SOCIAL MEDIA

In addition to sifting through the physical evidence found at their homes, investigators searched for digital clues to the brothers' lives. Both brothers had a prominent social media presence. Dzhokhar was an active Twitter user and also posted a profile on VKontakte, a Russian social media site similar to Facebook. Most of Dzhokhar's tweets were similar to those of any other American teenager. He tweeted about pop stars, TV shows, and movies, and he complained about pop-up ads on the Internet. He also occasionally sent messages that, at least in light of the Boston bombing, seemed much darker. In one, he wrote, "A decade in America already, I want out," and in another, "Never underestimate the rebel with a cause."[7] In one of his last tweets, sent at 1:43 a.m. on April 17, he said, "I'm a stress free kind of guy."[8]

Meanwhile, on Tamerlan's YouTube page, authorities found links to a number of videos featuring militant speakers. Included on Tamerlan's playlists was the heading "Terrorists," which included songs about jihad. In mainstream Islam, jihad simply means the struggle for a Muslim person to follow his or her religious duties. But followers of radical Islam often use the term to mean a violent war against non-Muslims. They also discovered an Amazon.com wish list that appeared to belong to Tamerlan. It included books about making friends, forging documents, and Chechen history.

Dzhokhar graduated in 2011, winning a $2,500 college scholarship from the City of Cambridge. The next year marked another milestone for Dzhokhar, as he was granted American citizenship on September 11, 2012.

After high school, Dzhokhar enrolled in the University of Massachusetts Dartmouth as a nursing student. In college, the former star student began to struggle with his studies. He failed classes such as Principles of Modern Chemistry, Intro to American Politics, and Chemistry and the Environment. He did better in Critical Writing, in which he earned a B.

## Difficult Adjustment

Unlike Dzhokhar, Tamerlan struggled to fit into his new homeland, perhaps because he was older when he moved to the United States and did not have a chance to make friends or learn English before he was thrust into high school. As a student in the Cambridge Rindge and Latin School's English as a Second Language Program, Tamerlan spent most of his time with other international students. Still, he had few friends. "I don't have a single American friend," he once said. "I don't understand them."[9]

Tamerlan, *left*, became a well-known amateur boxer.

When he was not at school, Tamerlan could often be found in the gym where he practiced boxing, a sport he had taken up in Dagestan. Tamerlan's fighting style was different from that of most American boxers. He stood with his legs straight, rather than crouching, and often threw gymnastics moves such as splits or handstands into his fights. Eventually, even his clothing became showy, earning him a reputation as arrogant. He would show up at tournaments wearing wild outfits, such as leather pants and a silk scarf, tight jeans with silver shoes and a trench coat, or white fur and snakeskin.

In 2009, Tamerlan won the New England Golden Gloves heavyweight championship and went on to compete at the national tournament in Salt Lake City, Utah. Although he fought well and some audience members thought he should have won in the finals, the winner of a boxing match is often determined by the judges. They awarded the championship to Tamerlan's opponent. Disappointed, Tamerlan decided to try again the next year. In 2010, he again won the New England Golden Gloves heavyweight championship. But Golden Gloves of America, the organization that sponsored the fight, had changed its policy and no longer allowed noncitizens to fight in its national championship.

Being barred from the fight seemed to change the course of Tamerlan's life. He quit boxing altogether. Around the same time, he dropped out of community college. He struggled with money problems. In 2009, a girlfriend had entered a domestic violence complaint against him, saying he had hit her. He worried the incident might keep him from attaining citizenship, but the charges were later dismissed.

In June 2010, Tamerlan married an American woman named Katherine Russell. Katherine converted to Islam, and the couple had a daughter, Zahira.

Tamerlan stayed home to care for the child while Katherine worked as a home health aide.

## A Strong Influence

According to friends and family members, Dzhokhar and Tamerlan were always close. The two often spent time together and were known in their neighborhood for throwing parties. Even after Dzhokhar entered college and Tamerlan married, Dzhokhar would sometimes spend the night at his brother's house.

Dzhokhar also seemed to look up to his big brother. An uncle later said that Tamerlan manipulated Dzhokhar, and a cousin said he warned Dzhokhar to stay away from his brother, who he thought would lead the younger boy into trouble. After the bombing, authorities began wondering if that was indeed what had happened.

### KATHERINE RUSSELL

Katherine Russell met Tamerlan Tsarnaev while she was a student at Suffolk University, and the two began to date. Although Katherine had grown up Christian, she converted to Islam and even began to cover her head with a hijab, or scarf, in public. In June 2010, the couple was married in a Muslim ceremony. Her family members said they did not believe Katherine was forced to convert but that she chose to do so. After the bombing, police investigated whether Katherine had known about or played any role in the bombing. As of August 2013, she had not been charged with any crime.

# CHAPTER
# SIX

# BECOMING RADICAL

Around the time Tamerlan quit boxing and dropped out of college, his mother, Zubeidat Tsarnaeva, urged him to turn to his religion for comfort. "I told Tamerlan that we are Muslim, and we are not practicing our religion, and how can we call ourselves Muslims?" Tsarnaeva told reporters.[1] Both Tamerlan and his mother became more devout. According to neighbors, the change was dramatic. He gave up smoking and drinking, put away the showy clothes, and grew a beard. His mother began to cover herself.

Tamerlan also began to read about Islam, pray, and attend various mosques, including the Islamic Society of Boston, a mosque near his home in Cambridge. The mosque's teachings did not seem to be conservative enough for Tamerlan, though. On one occasion, he interrupted prayers to denounce references to celebrating American secular holidays such as

Tamerlan attended the Islamic Society of Boston after dropping out of college.

## DENOUNCING THE BOMBINGS

The fact the Tsarnaevs were Muslim, led many people to worry about prejudice against other Muslims. "When one member of our [Muslim] community commits a heinous act, all of us are blamed," said writer Wajahat Ali.[2] To head off such prejudice, many Muslim leaders spoke out against the attacks both in the media and in their sermons.

Thanksgiving or Independence Day. Another time, he interrupted a sermon comparing Martin Luther King Jr. to the Prophet Muhammad. He even went into a Middle Eastern grocery store to confront a Muslim shopkeeper selling Thanksgiving turkeys.

Anzor Tsarnaev did not embrace his family's newfound devotion to Islam. In 2011, he and Zubeidat separated. Soon afterward, Anzor moved back to Dagestan. Dzhokhar missed his father and began to look to his brother as a father figure. Even so, he did not become a devout follower of Islam as his brother had. He continued to eat pork, something forbidden by Islam. He did not regularly attend a mosque, although he occasionally went to Friday prayers with Tamerlan. But at least one friend noticed a change in Dzhokhar. Shortly before the bombing, the friend remembered, Dzhokhar said, "God is all that matters. . . . When it comes to school . . . you can cheat easily. But when it comes to going to heaven, you can't cheat."[3]

## A Russian Tip

By early 2011, Tamerlan's lifestyle had caught the attention of officials in Russia, who contacted the FBI. The Russians reported Tamerlan might be a follower of radical Islam and that he had changed dramatically since 2010. Russian officials had learned Tamerlan planned

## LOST AND ANGRY BOYS?

Although Dzhokhar claimed he and his brother carried out their attack because of their passion for radical Islam, some authorities doubted the authenticity of that passion. Some noted that although Tamerlan claimed to be a devoted Muslim, he often slept in, which would keep him from participating in morning prayers. They also noted that although the brothers claimed to be angry with the United States, Tamerlan had applied for citizenship, and Dzhokhar had actually become a citizen. "They're angry kids with a veneer of ideology that's about skin-deep," said Philip Mudd, a former CIA and FBI counterterrorism official.[4]

Other experts pointed to Tamerlan's failed dreams as a possible motive for the attacks. "People who fail sometimes latch onto a cause that makes their anger legitimate," said Ronald Schouten, a psychiatrist specializing in terrorism.[5] And many pointed out that the brothers may have been searching for a sense of identity. "I think there's often a sense of divided loyalties . . . are you American first or are you Muslim first? And also of proving yourself as a man of action," said terrorism expert Brian Fishman.[6]

to travel to Dagestan in early 2012, and they were concerned he might be planning to join underground groups there. The FBI checked its databases and interviewed Tamerlan and his family but found no indication he was involved in terrorist activity. Although the FBI conveyed its findings to Russian officials, Russia contacted the US Central Intelligence Agency (CIA) in September 2011 with the same request to look into Tamerlan's activities. The CIA also found nothing that made them believe Tamerlan was a threat.

Although both the FBI and the CIA asked Russia for further information on what had prompted the requests, they did not receive a response. Only after the bombing did Russia authorities indicate their request was driven by an intercepted phone call in which Tamerlan discussed jihad with his mother, who had returned to live in Dagestan. Russian authorities also intercepted another call between Zubeidat and another person, also discussing jihad.

## Radical Ties?

After the bombing, investigators in both the United States and Russia attempted to put together a picture of what Tamerlan had done during his trip to Dagestan,

The brothers' mother maintained her sons' innocence.

where he had arrived in January 2012. Their main concern was discovering whether he had been radicalized—led to follow the radical strain of Islam that promotes jihad. They also wanted to know if any organized terrorist groups had helped in planning or carrying out the bombing.

Russian security forces had kept an eye on Tamerlan while he was in Dagestan. After the bombing, they reported Tamerlan had met with Makhmud Nidal, an Islamic militant, several times before Russian security forces killed Nidal in May. He also attended a mosque that followed the Salafist sect of Islam, criticized by some as supporting a strict, radical interpretation of the Koran. In July 2012, Tamerlan returned to the United

States. He applied for citizenship, but his application was delayed due to the earlier FBI investigation.

## Self-Radicalized?

In light of what authorities learned about Tamerlan's trip to Dagestan, some concluded he had been radicalized there and as a result returned to the United States determined to carry out an attack. Others believed Tamerlan had actually adopted radical ideas well before his trip. They said he had become self-radicalized through online sources. Tamerlan's YouTube page included videos of Salafi preacher Sheik Feiz Mohammed. Both Tamerlan and his brother also listened to the sermons of Islamic militant Anwar al-Awlaki.

As authorities debated how the Tsarnaevs became radicalized, they also wondered what had motivated their attacks. Written on the inside of the boat where Dzhokhar had hidden from authorities, investigators found a note indicating the attack was revenge for the US involvement in the Iraq War (2003–2011) and the War in Afghanistan (2001–). "When you attack one Muslim, you attack all Muslims," the note said.[7] Later, when Dzhokhar was able to communicate with investigators, he repeated the same idea, saying that he and his brother were jihadists. Dzhokhar also indicated the brothers had acted alone, with no outside help or training.

## Making a Plan

According to Dzhokhar, the brothers originally planned to carry out their attack on July 4. Records showed Tamerlan purchased fireworks—possibly so the brothers could use the black powder for bombs—on February 6, 2013. Then, the two began assembling their bombs, working in Tamerlan's apartment. The bombs were made from pressure cookers filled with nails, ball bearings, and black powder. They were designed to be set off by remote control.

The brothers finished their bombs more quickly than expected and decided to move their target from July 4 to Patriots' Day. They scoped out the marathon course and decided the finish line would be the ideal location for their attack.

### ADDITIONAL ATTACKS

Law enforcement officials found additional bombs in the Tsarnaevs' homes and in the stolen SUV. Dzhokhar confirmed he and his brother had planned more attacks, saying they had decided to bring the rest of their bombs to Times Square in New York City. Authorities did not believe the brothers had a specific plan for setting off the explosives.

# CHAPTER
# SEVEN

# SEEKING JUSTICE

When police apprehended Dzhokhar, they did not read him his Miranda rights, which advise a person under arrest that he or she has the right to remain silent. Miranda rights usually have to be read to a person who has been arrested, but in Dzhokhar's case, authorities decided to use the public safety exception to the Miranda rule. This exception can be used when authorities believe they need immediate answers from a subject regarding threats to public safety—such as plans for additional attacks.

Any questions for Dzhokhar would have to wait, though. After his capture, he was rushed to the hospital with gunshot wounds to his head, neck, legs, and hand. For the first day after his attack, he remained unconscious. Counterterrorism agents waited outside his hospital room, ready to question him the moment he woke. They finally had their chance on Sunday, April 21. Although Dzhokhar's neck wound kept him from speaking, he wrote his answers to the

After being captured, Dzhokhar was checked for explosives and given immediate medical attention.

## AN EARLIER CRIME

As authorities investigated the Boston Marathon bombing, they came to believe Tamerlan—and possibly Dzhokhar—had been involved in another crime two years earlier. On September 11, 2011, three people were murdered in Waltham, Massachusetts. They were found with their throats slashed and their bodies covered with marijuana. On May 22, 2013, an associate of Tamerlan's, Ibragim Todashev, said both he and Tamerlan were involved in the murders. He then allegedly tried to attack the FBI agents questioning him. The agents shot and killed Todashev.

investigator's questions. During the interrogation, Dzhokhar admitted he and his brother had carried out the bombing.

## Facing Charges

On Monday, April 22, Magistrate Judge Marianne B. Bowler met with Dzhokhar in his hospital room for a brief hearing. After reading him his Miranda rights, the judge read the charges against him: "using a weapon of mass destruction and malicious destruction of property by means of an explosive device."[1] The charges carried a possible sentence of death.

An affidavit filed with the charges outlined the evidence against Dzhokhar, including video footage that showed him placing the second bomb. According to the affidavit, surveillance video showed two men, whom investigators had identified as Tamerlan and Dzhokhar

The brothers, *top right*, were later spotted in many photographs taken by spectators near the finish line.

Tsarnaev, arriving on Boylston Street around 2:38 p.m. on the day of the marathon. Both carried large backpacks. At 2:45, Dzhokhar stopped on the sidewalk outside the Forum Restaurant and set his bag on the ground. Tamerlan had already proceeded farther down the street, closer to the finish line. Approximately five minutes later, the first bomb exploded near the finish line. Although nearly all of the spectators around him turned to look toward the sound of the explosion, Dzhokhar remained calm. Then he walked away from the Forum, in the opposite direction of the finish line, leaving his bag behind. Approximately ten seconds later, the second bomb exploded right where the bag had been left.[2]

After being told the charges against him, Dzhokhar continued recovering in the hospital. On Friday, April 26, he was doing well enough to be transferred to a medical detention center at Fort Devens, Massachusetts. In early June, Dzhokhar's mother reported she was able to talk to him for the first time since his arrest. He told her he was doing well and had received financial support from someone who had opened a bank account for him.

## Opposing Sides

Since Dzhokhar could not afford to hire an attorney, public defender Miriam Conrad was appointed to lead his defense team. Conrad had previously represented Richard Reid, a terrorist who had attempted to blow up an airplane in December 2001 using explosives hidden in his shoe. Judy Clarke, a San Diego lawyer experienced in capital cases, was also appointed to Dzhokhar's defense. Capital cases are those in which the defendant faces a possible sentence of execution. Clarke is known for getting notorious criminals—including Eric Rudolph, who set off a bomb at the 1996 Summer Olympics in Atlanta—life in prison instead of the death penalty.

Facing off against the defense would be an equally strong prosecution led by Carmen Ortiz, the US attorney for Massachusetts. US attorneys represent the

## DISAGREEMENTS OVER HOW TO PROCEED

After Dzhokhar was read his Miranda rights by Judge Bowler, he stopped answering investigators' questions. This frustrated the FBI as well as Republican lawmakers. They did not believe investigators had been given enough time to question the suspect thoroughly to ensure he had not been working as part of a larger terrorist group. However, a Justice Department spokesman said defendants must be informed of the right to remain silent during their initial appearance. Some lawyers and civil rights activists even felt that authorities had already waited too long to read Dzhokhar his rights.

There were also disagreements about how to proceed with the case. Some Republican lawmakers said Dzhokhar should be held as an enemy combatant. This would have allowed investigators to continue to question him without a lawyer, at least until they were certain he had no connections to Al Qaeda. Other lawmakers said it would be illegal to try the suspect, an American citizen, as an enemy combatant. They insisted the case could be handled successfully in civilian court and that intelligence could still be obtained from the suspect even if he had a lawyer present during questioning.

Carmen Ortiz, US attorney for Massachusetts since 2010, would lead the prosecution against Dzhokhar.

federal government in court cases. The first woman and first Hispanic US attorney in Massachusetts history, Ortiz had earned a reputation as a tough prosecutor.

## Future Trial

Putting together both the prosecution and defense for a high-profile capital case takes time, and Dzhokhar's trial was not expected to be held until several years after the actual bombing. In the meantime, lawyers around the country debated whether the trial would be held in Boston. In general, trials are held in the state where the crime occurred unless a judge decides a defendant cannot get a fair trial there. Dzhokhar's lawyers could seek to have the trial moved, arguing it would be impossible to find an impartial jury in Boston. The prosecution, however, might request the case be tried in Boston because most of the witnesses lived in or around the Boston area.

Wherever the trial would be held, many felt the prosecution had a strong case. In the days after his arrest, Dzhokhar had confessed to taking part in the bombings. Since this confession was made before Dzhokhar had been read his Miranda rights, however, there were questions over whether the prosecution would be able to use it in court. It would be up to a judge to decide how much—if any—of what Dzhokhar had said in the first two days after his arrest could be used as evidence against him. Even without the confession, however, many experts believed prosecutors could make their case. Video footage showed Dzhokhar leaving behind a backpack in the location of the second explosion. In addition, officers who had taken part in the shootout and capture of Dzhokhar could be called as witnesses. Investigators had also found physical evidence linking Dzhokhar to the crime, including fireworks and a black jacket and white hat—the same type of clothing

## THE DEATH PENALTY

Massachusetts is one of 18 states in the United States that does not allow the death penalty. However, acts of terrorism, including the bombing of public places, are treated by the government as federal crimes rather than state ones. Federal crimes can carry a penalty of death, regardless of where they are perpetrated. According to a poll published May 1, 2013, 70 percent of Americans supported the use of the death penalty in Dzhokhar's case.[3]

the suspect in the surveillance video wore.

The most difficult decision for the prosecution would likely be whether or not to seek the death penalty, a decision that would ultimately lie with the US attorney general. The attorney general is the head of the US Department of Justice and is considered the top law enforcement official and lawyer in the United States. If the government approved a capital case, it would be the job of Dzhokhar's lawyers to keep him alive. To do so, the defense team might focus on mitigating circumstances that could provide a reason to spare Dzhokhar's life despite his involvement in the bombing. As former federal prosecutor David Raskin explained, "Was he mentally ill? Was he just blindly following his brother? Was his childhood particularly traumatic? These questions don't go to guilt or innocence, but could be central to what ultimately happens here."[4] Some lawyers predicted the defense would highlight Dzhokhar's youth, the influence of his older brother, and his previous academic, social, and athletic accomplishments.

Instead of going to trial, some legal experts believed Dzhokhar would strike a plea agreement with prosecutors. In a plea agreement, a defendant agrees to plead guilty and cooperate with authorities in return for a less harsh sentence. In Dzhokhar's case, a plea agreement might mean pleading guilty in return for a sentence of life in prison. If investigators found evidence that Dzhokhar was involved with a foreign terrorist group, the prosecution might also offer a plea agreement to convince him to share that information. However, on July 10, 2013, Dzhokhar pled not guilty on all charges.

# CHAPTER
# EIGHT

# NEW TERROR THREATS AND PUBLIC POLICY

Immediately after the attacks of September 11, 2001, authorities at all levels of government instituted numerous counterterrorism measures. Airports, train stations, and other high-traffic places added security. Officials monitored potentially threatening communications. Emergency plans were drawn up, and disaster drills were practiced. All of these measures made it difficult for terrorist organizations to carry out another large-scale attack.

## The Homegrown Threat

The Boston Marathon bombing represented a relatively new threat: the homegrown terrorist. These attacks are carried out by people already living in the targeted country. Homegrown terror attacks are generally

Many airports introduced full-body scanners as a response to the threat of terrorist attacks.

## HOMEGROWN PLOTS

According to the Congressional Research Service, there were 63 homegrown jihadist plots or attacks in the United States between September 11, 2001, and January 2013. The majority occurred between 2009 and 2012. Some terrorism experts saw this as a sign of the increasing threat of homegrown attacks. But others said that based on the number of terrorism arrests, the threat was actually declining. In 2011, 21 people were accused of plotting jihadist terrorist attacks. That was down to 14 in 2012.[2]

smaller in scale than organized plots such as the attacks on September 11, 2001. The Boston bombing killed three, whereas nearly 3,000 were killed on September 11, 2001.[1]

However, homegrown attacks appeal to terrorists for a number of reasons. Like the Tsarnaev brothers, many homegrown terrorists are radicalized and trained online. In addition, the materials needed to carry out such attacks are generally easy to obtain, and they do not typically raise red flags to authorities. Anyone can purchase nails, pressure cookers, or fireworks. Small-scale attacks can be relatively easy to carry out, too, especially at events with little security. In the Tsarnaevs' case, there were no gates, metal detectors, or other security devices to get past at the Boston Marathon.

## Lone Wolves

According to law enforcement officials and others, small-scale attacks are often even more difficult to stop than coordinated large-scale attacks. "The one thing that we can be reasonably sure of is, [terrorists] are not going to do the same thing two times in a row, which makes protecting the public that much more challenging," said New York Mayor Michael Bloomberg.[3]

One of the hardest parts about stopping homegrown terrorists is figuring out who they are ahead of time. Authorities often refer to them as lone wolves because they act on their own. Investigators cannot intercept potentially incriminating communications between lone wolves and others regarding an upcoming attack because there often are none.

### ALERTING AUTHORITIES

For more than 20 years, the FBI has relied on a tripwire system to help identify people who might be making a bomb. Through this system, those who sell materials that could be used in a bomb are trained to alert authorities of anyone making a suspicious purchase. Items monitored have included fertilizer, used to make the explosives in the 1995 Oklahoma City bombing, and certain materials used in chemical-based bombs. After the Boston Marathon bombing there was speculation that authorities could expand their tripwire system, perhaps to include fireworks or similar explosives.

In the wake of the Boston bombing, some authorities suggested closer ties between police and the Muslim community could help to spot lone wolves before they become threats. Muslim community leaders might be able to inform police of those they suspect have become radicalized. Closer ties between Boston's Muslim community and police might have led Muslim leaders to go to police after Tamerlan's outbursts at the mosque, for example. Others said targeting the Muslim community for such efforts is unfair and that further research should be conducted into what drives people to extremist violence.

## The Cameras Are Watching

In addition to finding ways to identify attackers before they strike, lawmakers and law enforcement agents looked for new security measures that could make attacks harder to carry out. Since video footage proved vital in identifying the Boston Marathon bombers, many people advocated increased surveillance in public places. "Images from cameras do not lie. They do not forget. They can be viewed by a jury as evidence of what occurred," said Boston police commissioner Ed Davis.[4]

Cooperation between law enforcement and Muslim communities is seen as one way to prevent violence by Islamic extremists.

Other experts pointed out that in addition to identifying terrorists after an attack, cameras might actually deter some terrorists who fear getting caught. Some cameras, including many already installed in New York City by 2013, could even foil an attack by detecting a bag left behind in a public place. Other surveillance devices with special sensors may detect radioactive or chemical devices.

Privacy advocates, however, warned more surveillance could intrude on civil liberties. In 2007, the American Civil Liberties Union (ACLU), a group that strives to defend the individual rights guaranteed by the US Constitution, argued surveillance cameras were ineffective and governments should stop installing them. Despite the protests of the ACLU and others, most Americans seemed to be willing to give up privacy in the interest of security. A poll taken the week after the bombing showed that 78 percent of Americans approved of the use of surveillance cameras.[5]

## Other Security Measures

Part of the reason the Boston Marathon was such an attractive target was its size. Police could not possibly screen everyone who attended the race. In the wake of the attack, many organizations wondered how to improve security at marathons and other events that draw massive crowds.

Among the options discussed were securing the start and finish lines of races and perhaps even moving the finish line into a stadium, where access could be controlled. Others suggested conducting random searches of fans and deploying bomb-sniffing dogs

Crowded places, such as shopping malls, are seen as being vulnerable to terrorist attacks.

throughout a racecourse. Although the adoption of such measures would not prevent all attacks, it would "create a hostile environment" for attackers, according to Michael O'Neil, former commander of the New York Police Department's counterterrorism division.[6]

## Immigration Reform

The attack on the Boston Marathon occurred only days before the Senate Judiciary Committee was scheduled to begin hearings on an immigration reform bill. On Friday, April 19, as law enforcement hunted down

Dzhokhar, senators gathered to discuss the bill, which included border security changes as well as a provision that would allow immigrants who had entered the United States illegally to become citizens.

The bombing led some senators to question the immigration bill. They wondered if its security measures would be tough enough to stop people who wanted to harm Americans from entering the country and even becoming citizens. Others pointed out that tighter immigration security measures might not have stopped the Tsarnaevs from coming to the United States because they were only children when their family arrived. In addition, many believed the brothers adopted their radical beliefs while living in the United States. "You can't just say no one can ever come to the country," said Senator Lindsey Graham of South Carolina. "So, if they came here legally and they got radicalized, that's no different to me than being born here and getting radicalized."[7]

While senators debated the need for immigration reform and increased security, others pointed to the need to ensure immigrants were assimilated into their new lives in America. They said immigrants—especially those who arrive as children and teens—need to feel

Senator Graham criticized the government for prosecuting Dzhokhar as a US citizen rather than as an enemy combatant.

as though they are part of their new community. Many suggested the government, teachers, and communities should be involved in the assimilation process, from providing financial and other assistance to watching for warning signs a child is struggling, such as falling grades or increased isolation.

# CHAPTER
# NINE

# BOSTON STRONG

As the nation grappled with security and immigration issues, the people of Boston continued healing. In the days after the attack, many throughout the city adopted the slogan "Boston Strong."[1] The logo could be found on T-shirts, signs, and even Twitter avatars.

## A Community of Runners

The Boston Marathon impacted not only the city of Boston but also a worldwide community of runners, many of whom expressed commitment to the sport and to one another after the attacks. Bill Rodgers, a four-time winner of the Boston Marathon, summarized how many people felt about the race: "It's such a human sport. I don't think these bombers get that—that when they attack the Boston Marathon, they don't just attack America. They attack all the countries with runners in the marathon."[2]

Bombing responder Carlos Arredondo, *left*, appeared at a Boston Bruins game with bombing victim Jeff Bauman, *center*, in June 2013.

87

Runners in the London Marathon observed a 30-second silence before the race in remembrance of the Boston victims.

The London Marathon was held on Sunday, April 21, only six days after the Boston Marathon bombing. Many of the 36,000 runners wore black ribbons in honor of Boston victims, and spectators waved American flags.[3] Shorter races in honor of Boston victims were held in New York, Missouri, California, Vermont, Michigan, and other locations across the United States and the world. Many of the organizers of these races collected donations for bombing victims.

Runners did not shy away from events in Boston either. On May 8, the Boston Athletic Association opened registration for a 10K race scheduled for June. It would be the first race in Boston since the marathon bombing. Within 13 hours, registration had to be closed because the race was full. Thousands had signed up to run. And on May 25, 3,000 people—many of whom had run in the Boston Marathon—gathered to run or walk the last mile (1.6 km) of the marathon in an event known as OneRun.[4]

## Long Road

By early May, some of those most severely wounded in the attacks began to be released from the hospital. On June 3, Erika Brannock became the last victim to leave the hospital. The 29-year-old had undergone 11 surgeries during her seven-week hospital stay. One leg had been amputated above the knee, but doctors had been able to save her other leg.

Even after all of the victims were released from the hospital, many knew they would need additional surgeries down the road. Some even faced the possibility of future amputation if their recovery did not proceed as doctors hoped.

Those who had lost limbs or suffered severe shrapnel injuries in the bombing moved from hospitals into rehabilitation centers where they could continue their recovery. Many were admitted to Spaulding Rehabilitation Hospital in Boston, where they learned to walk with crutches or prostheses.

In addition to their physical rehabilitation, many patients also had to deal with the emotional trauma of being injured in the attack. At Spaulding, patients had access to mental-health counselors. Many patients also found it comforting to be continuing their recovery

## ADVANCES IN PROSTHETICS

Since 2001, nearly 1,600 US service members have faced amputations as a result of injuries sustained during the wars in Iraq and Afghanistan.[5] With so many people now needing prosthetic limbs, the field of prosthetics has advanced rapidly. Today, prosthetics are generally made of carbon fiber, a strong, lightweight material. In addition, many prosthetics include microprocessors in the knees and ankles. These computer chips use information about the position of the leg to adjust for the next step. For double amputees, wireless technology can allow one prosthetic leg to communicate with the other to adjust stride and speed. In addition, some prostheses can be controlled by contracting the muscles in the stump of the limb. By 2012, scientists were also working on technology that would enable amputees to move their prosthetic limb just by thinking about it.

Doctors predicted someday there would even be sensors that would enable amputees to feel sensations from their prosthetic devices as they would from real limbs. "The technology we have today is good," said Hugh Herr, founder of prosthetics company iWalk. "In a decade, it will be extraordinary, and in 20 years, it will be unimaginable."[6]

with other bombing victims. "There is a bond. It's like there are some things that I can share with the group that I can't share with my family, because you've got to be strong for them," said bombing survivor Beth Roche, whose leg was seriously wounded in the attack.[7]

## Covering the Expenses

The toll on bombing survivors was not only physical and psychological—it was also financial. Weeks in hospitals and rehabilitation centers added up to thousands of dollars in medical bills for many. In addition, amputees faced the cost of prosthetic legs, which could range from $7,000 to $90,000 or more.[8] Although many victims had insurance, they worried it would not be enough to cover their expenses. In addition, some who had been roofers or performed other physical labor would have to find new jobs after the attacks. Others faced the cost of modifying their cars or homes to fit their new needs.

Americans responded to the attacks in Boston with an outpouring of generosity. Many gave money to One Fund Boston, which was set up to collect donations for bombing victims. By July, the fund had collected more than $60 million.[9] The families of those killed as well as victims who had suffered permanent brain damage

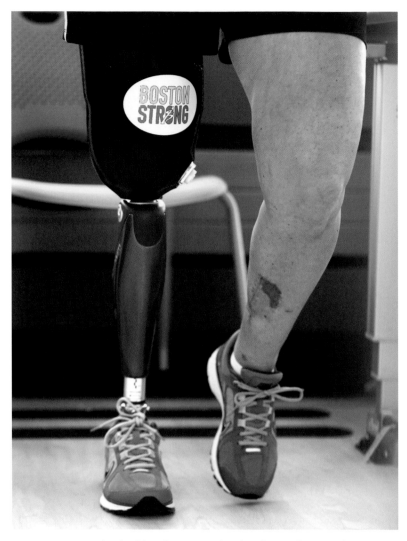
Many victims who had lost legs were fitted with prosthetic replacements.

or lost limbs received the highest compensation from the fund.

Family and friends of many of those injured in the attacks also turned to crowdsourcing fund-raising Web sites to raise money for their recovery. These sites, such as GiveForward or GoFundMe, allow people to set up pages to collect donations for specific victims. They also allow donors to post words of encouragement, while victims can post updates on their recovery. These types of fund-raisers brought in hundreds of thousands of dollars for some victims.

As those injured in the attacks continued their recovery, there were signs of healing in Boston. Throughout the month of May, a number of marathon bombing survivors were invited to throw out ceremonial first pitches at Boston Red Sox games. Among them were Heather Abbott, who lost her left leg; Peter DiMartino, who suffered burns and shrapnel wounds; and Jeff Bauman Jr., who had both legs amputated after the attack. On May 28, 18-year-old bombing survivor Sydney Corcoran was crowned prom queen at her high school. On May 31, the University of

## BOSTON STRONG CONCERT

On May 30, thousands of people, including many survivors of the bombing, turned out for the Boston Strong Concert. The five and a half hour show included performances by the bands Aerosmith, New Kids on the Block, Boston, and Boyz II Men. It raised an estimated $1.5 million for the One Fund Boston, although critics said it could have raised more if it had been televised.[10]

Massachusetts Boston presented a posthumous bachelor's degree to Krystle Campbell, who had been a student there from 2005 to 2007.

## Ready to Run Again

The majority of those who were at the 2013 Boston Marathon vowed to return the next year. Race organizers agreed to give the more than 5,000 people who had not been able to cross the finish line in 2013 entry into the 2014 marathon.[11] Others who had never attempted the marathon before were also determined to join runners there. Among them was Adrianne Haslet-Davis, a dancer who lost her left foot in the bombing.

Dick Traum, who in 1976 became the first amputee to run a marathon, invited those who had been injured in the bombing to join a group of disabled runners called Achilles International in the 2014 Boston Marathon. Whether they ran or used a wheelchair, Traum said participating in the marathon would allow the bombing victims to "slay the monster."[12]

Desisa, *right*, met with US Secretary of State John Kerry, *left*, at the US Embassy in Ethiopia.

After the attack, Lelisa Desisa, the men's winner of the 2013 Boston Marathon, donated his first-place medal to the people of Boston and pledged to run alongside them in the 2014 race. "Sport holds the power to unify people," he said. "We will return to Boston to show the world that our commitment to sport, our commitment to our freedom is stronger than any act of violence."[14]

# TIMELINE

## 1986

Tamerlan Tsarnaev is born in Russia; the family soon moves to Kyrgyzstan and also lives briefly in Chechnya.

## 1993

Dzhokhar Tsarnaev is born.

## 1999

The Tsarnaev family moves to Dagestan.

## 2002

Dzhokhar and his father move to the United States.

## 2003

Tamerlan moves with the rest of the family to the United States.

## 2010

In June, Tamerlan marries American Katherine Russell, who converts to Islam.

## 2011

Russian authorities ask the FBI and CIA to
look into Tamerlan, but the agencies find
no evidence he is a potential terrorist.

## 2011

Dzhokhar graduates from Cambridge
Rindge and Latin School and enrolls in the
University of Massachusetts Dartmouth.

## 2012

In January, Tamerlan travels to Dagestan,
where he remains for six months.

## 2012

Dzhokhar becomes a US citizen on September 11.

## 2013

At 2:50 p.m. on April 15, two explosions near the finish
line of the Boston Marathon kill 3 and injure 264.

## 2013

On April 17, investigators identify two suspects
in video footage from the bombing.

# TIMELINE

## 2013
Authorities release the suspects' pictures to the public on April 18.

## 2013
At 10:20 p.m. on April 18, Tamerlan and Dzhokhar allegedly shoot and kill MIT police officer Sean Collier and hijack an SUV.

## 2013
After a car chase, police shoot and kill Tamerlan Tsarnaev in the city of Watertown, Massachusetts, around 1:00 a.m. on April 19.

## 2013
The Boston area is under lockdown as police search for Dzhokhar on April 19; he is apprehended around 8:30 p.m.

## 2013
On April 21, Dzhokhar is questioned without being read his Miranda rights and admits to taking part in the bombing.

## 2013

On April 22, Dzhokhar is charged with using a weapon of mass destruction and malicious destruction of property by means of an explosive device.

## 2013

Boston's Boylston Street—the site of the explosions—reopens on April 24.

## 2013

On April 26, Dzhokhar is transferred to a medical detention center at Fort Devens, Massachusetts.

## 2013

On May 25, 3,000 people walk or run the last mile of the Boston Marathon in an event known as OneRun.

## 2013

The final bombing victim is released from the hospital on June 3.

# ESSENTIAL FACTS

## Date of Event
April 15, 2013

## Place of Event
Boylston Street in Boston, Massachusetts

## Key Players
- The bombers, Tamerlan and Dzhokhar Tsarnaev

- The victims who died, Martin Richard, Krystle Campbell, Lu Lingzi, Sean Collier, and many others who were injured.

- Bystanders, emergency personnel, and doctors who responded instantly at the scene, saving many lives

- Richard DesLauriers, the FBI agent in charge of the investigation

## Highlights of Event
- On April 15, 2013, more than 23,000 people ran in the Boston Marathon. At 2:50 p.m., just over four hours into the race, a bomb exploded near the finish line. A second bomb exploded ten seconds later.

- Authorities relied on pictures and video footage captured by spectators, surveillance cameras, and media to identify two suspects. On April 18, they released the suspects' images to the public.

- After allegedly killing MIT police officer Sean Collier, the suspects led police on a car chase that ended in Watertown, Massachusetts, with a shootout. One suspect, whom authorities identified as Tamerlan Tsarnaev, was shot and killed. His brother, Dzhokhar, escaped.

- On April 19, the Boston area was put under lockdown as police searched for Dzhokhar. Around 8:30 p.m., Dzhokhar was apprehended and taken to a hospital.

- On April 21, Dzhokhar was questioned without being read his Miranda rights under the public safety exception to the Miranda Rule. He admitted to authorities that he and Tamerlan had carried out the bombing.

- On April 22, a federal judge read Dzhokhar his Miranda rights. She also read the charges against him: using a weapon of mass destruction and malicious destruction of property by means of an explosive device.

- On June 3, the last injured survivor of the bombing was released from the hospital.

## Quote

"Sport holds the power to unify people. We will return to Boston to show the world that our commitment to sport, our commitment to our freedom is stronger than any act of violence." —*Lelisa Desisa, 2013 men's winner, Boston Marathon*

# GLOSSARY

**affidavit**
A written document sworn under oath to be true.

**assimilate**
To fit into a new culture or community.

**civilian**
Having to do with someone who is not a member of the military.

**ethnic**
Describing someone who belongs to a group with a common racial, national, or religious heritage, but is living outside the boundaries of that group.

**ideology**
A system of beliefs held by a person or group.

**impartial**
Not prejudiced; treating everyone equally.

**Koran**
The holy book of Islam, which Muslims believe contains the words of God to the prophet Muhammad.

**mitigating circumstances**
In law, circumstances, such as age or mental illness, that are taken into consideration when determining the severity of the charges or punishment a defendant faces.

**posthumous**
Occurring after someone has died.

### pressure cooker
A metal pot used to cook food quickly using steam under high pressure.

### public defender
A government-paid lawyer appointed to defend those who cannot afford a lawyer.

### radical
Supporting an extreme view or interpretation of a religion or political idea that differs markedly from the views of others.

### Soviet Union
A former communist country in eastern Europe and northern Asia that included Russia and other republics and broke apart into separate nations in 1991.

### tourniquet
A bandage, piece of cloth, or other device tied around a limb to stop blood loss from a wound.

### triage
The sorting of patients based on their need for treatment.

# ADDITIONAL RESOURCES

## Selected Bibliography

Bronner, Ethan, Charlie Savage, and William K. Rashbaum. "Legal Questions Riddle Boston Marathon Case." *New York Times*. New York Times, 20 Apr. 2013. Web. 29 May 2013.

Patriquin, Martin, Jonathon Gatehouse, Michael Friscolanti, Luiza Savage, Rosemary Westwood. "Boston Bleeds." *Maclean's*. MacLean's, 29 Apr. 2013. Web. 14 May 2013.

## Further Readings

Miller, Debra A. *Terrorism*. Detroit, MI: Lucent Books/Gale Cengage Learning, 2008. Print.

*World Book Focus on Terrorism*. Chicago, MI: World Book, 2003. Print.

## Web Sites

To learn more about the Boston Marathon bombing, visit ABDO Publishing Company online at **www.abdopublishing.com**. Web sites about the Boston Marathon bombing are featured on our Book Links page. These links are routinely monitored and updated to provide the most current information available.

## Places to Visit

### Boston Athletic Association

1 Ash Street
Hopkinton, MA 01748
508-435-6905
http://www.baa.org/
The Boston Athletic Association (BAA) organizes the Boston
Marathon. Its registration office is located in Hopkinton,
where the race begins. The BAA also sponsors a running
club, youth programs, and additional races. The office is
open weekdays.

### Boston Common

139 Tremont Street
Boston, MA 02111
617-536-4100 x888
http://thefreedomtrail.org/freedom-trail/boston-common.
shtml
Each year, those running in the Boston Marathon gather at
Boston Common before boarding buses to the starting line.
Located in the center of Boston, Boston Common is the
oldest public park in the United States. It is also the starting
point of the Freedom Trail, which leads past 16 of the city's
historical sites.

# SOURCE NOTES

## Chapter 1. From Triumph to Tragedy

1. Abby Ohlheiser. "The Significance of Patriots' Day." *Slate*. Slate, 15 Apr. 2013. Web. 29 July 2013.

2. JD Hale. "A Personal Account of Being at the Finish Line." *Yankee*. Yankee, Apr. 2013. Web. 29 July 2013.

3. "2013 Statistics." *Boston Athletic Association*. Boston Athletic Association, 23 May 2013. Web. 29 July 2013.

4. John Eligon and Michael Cooper. "Blasts at Boston Marathon Kill 3 and Injure 100." *New York Times*. New York Times, 15 Apr. 2013. Web. 22 May 2013.

5. "Explore the Course." *Boston.com*. Boston.com, 2013. Web. 29 July 2013.

6. Barbara Huebner. "Rita Jeptoo Wins 2013 Boston Marathon." *Boston Athletic Association*. Boston Athletic Association, 22 Apr. 2013. Web. 29 July 2013.

7. "The B.A.A.'s Official Charity Program for the Boston Marathon." *Boston Athletic Association*. Boston Athletic Association, 2013. Web. 29 July 2013.

8. Jonathon Gatehouse and Martin Patriquin. "Boston Bleeds." *Maclean's*. Maclean's, 20 Apr. 2013. Web. 29 July 2013.

9. "Guide to the Bombing at the Boston Marathon." *Newsworks*. Associated Press, 16 Apr. 2013. Web. 29 July 2013.

## Chapter 2. Rapid Response

1. Tim Rohan. "In Grisly Image, a Father Sees His Son." *New York Times*. New York Times, 16 Apr. 2013. Web. 29 July 2013.

2. "Boston Marathon Bomb Damage Worse Than Thought: 264 Seriously Injured, 14 Lost Limbs." *Washington Times*. Washington Times, 23 Apr. 2013. Web. 29 July 2013.

3. Doug Belkin, Andrew Grossman, and Kevin Clark. "Emergency Planning, Speed Saved Lives After the Boston Marathon Attack." *Wall Street Journal*. Wall Street Journal, 16 Apr. 2013. Web. 23 May 2013.

4. Cameron McWhirter, Tamer El-Ghobashy, and David Roman. "Authorities Hone Fight Against Terrorism." *Wall Street Journal*. Wall Street Journal, 17 Apr. 2013. Web. 22 May 2013.

5. "Obama Transcript: 'We Will Find Out Who Did This.'" *Wall Street Journal*. Wall Street Journal, 15 Apr. 2013. Web. 29 July 2013.

## Chapter 3. The Manhunt

1. "Boston Bombing Survivor Spotted Suspect in Crowd." *Portland Press Herald*. Portland Press Herald, 26 Apr. 2013. Web. 29 July 2013.

2. Katharine Q. Seelye, Eric Schmitt, and Scott Shane. "Boston Bombs Were Loaded to Maim." *New York Times*. New York Times, 16 Apr. 2013. Web. 22 May 2013.

3. "Rick Deslaurier, FBI Special Agent Speaks at Press Conference about the Boston Marathon Bombings." *FDCH*. FDCH Political Transcripts, 18 Apr. 2013. *Newspaper Source Plus*. Web. 30 May 2013.

4. Ibid.

5. Katharine Q. Seelye and Ian Lovett. "After Attack, Suspects Returned to Routines, Raising No Suspicions." *New York Times*. New York Times, 26 Apr. 2013. Web. 21 May 2013.

6. S. L. Price. "Boston Stands As One." *Sports Illustrated*. Sports Illustrated, 29 Apr. 2013. *MasterFILE Premier*. Web. 22 May 2013.

7. Michael Wines and Katharine Q. Seelye. "After Boston Attack, 3 Friends Covered It Up, Prosecutors Say." *New York Times*. New York Times, 1 May 2013. Web. 29 July 2013.

8. Melissa Gray. "Police Chief: Boston Manhunt Began with Intense Firefight in Dark Street." *CNN*. CNN, 22 Apr. 2013. Web. 29 July 2013.

9. "Second Boston Marathon Bombing Suspect Dzhokhar Tsarnaev in Custody." *PBS News Hour*. PBS, 19 Apr. 2013. Web. 29 July 2013.

10. Scott Shane. "Bombings End Decade of Strikingly Few Successful Terrorism Attacks in U.S." *New York Times*. New York Times, 16 Apr. 2013. Web. 29 July 2013.

11. Chelsea J. Carter and Greg Botelho. "'CAPTURED!!!' Boston Police Announce Marathon Bombing Suspect in Custody." *CNN*. CNN, 19 Apr. 2013. Web. 29 July 2013.

## Chapter 4. Saying Good-bye

1. Erin Delmore. "'You Will Run Again,' Obama Promises Boston at Interfaith Service." *NBC News*. NBC News, 18 Apr. 2013. Web. 29 July 2013.

2. "The Boston Victims." *New York Times*. New York Times, 20 Apr. 2013. Web. 29 July 2013.

3. Christine McConville. "Tearful Goodbye for Boston Marathon Bombing Victim Krystle Campbell." *Boston Herald*. Boston Herald, 23 Apr. 2013. Web. 29 July 2013.

4. Jess Bidgood. "Hundreds Gather at Services Held for Marathon Victims." *New York Times*. New York Times, 22 Apr. 2013. Web. 29 July 2013.

5. Ibid.

6. Ibid.

7. Ibid.

8. Alicia Dennis, et al. "Horror at the Marathon: Tales of Chaos and Courage." *People*. People, 29 Apr. 2013. *MasterFILE Premier*. Web. 17 May 2013.

9. Jess Bidgood. "On a Field at M.I.T., 10,000 Remember an Officer Who Was Killed." *New York Times*. New York Times, 24 Apr. 2013. Web. 29 July 2013.

10. Ibid.

11. "Sean Collier's Body Brought Home." *CNN Transcripts*. CNN, 20 Apr. 2013. Web. 29 July 2013.

12. Jake Tapper and Matt Smith. "Source: Boston Bomb Suspect Says Brother Was Brains behind Attack." *CNN*. CNN, 22 Apr. 2013. Web. 29 July 2013.

13. Brent Forester. "Boston Marathon Runner & Psychiatrist Shares Personal Story of Patriots' Day 2013." *American Psychiatric Association*. American Psychiatric Association, 29 Apr. 2013. Web. 29 July 2013.

14. Jonathon Gatehouse and Martin Patriquin. "Boston Bleeds." *Maclean's*. Maclean's, 20 Apr. 2013. Web. 29 July 2013.

15. Thomas L. Friedman. "Bring On the Next Marathon." *New York Times*. New York Times, 16 Apr. 2013. Web. 29 July 2013.

16. Leon Wieseltier. "Don't Move On: The Boston Massacre and Our Emotional Efficiency." *New Republic*. New Republic, 24 Apr. 2013. Web. 29 July 2013.

## Chapter 5. The Tsarnaev Brothers

1. Scott Shane. "Suspects With Foot in 2 Worlds, Perhaps Echoing Plots of Past." *New York Times*. New York Times, 20 Apr. 2013. Web. 29 July 2013.

2. Ibid.

# SOURCE NOTES CONTINUED

3. Michael Wines. "The Dark Side, Carefully Masked." *New York Times*. New York Times, 4 May 2013. Web. 30 May 2013.

4. Ibid

5. Alan Cullison, Paul Sonne, Anton Troianovski, and David George-Cosh. "Turn to Religion Split Suspects' Home." *Wall Street Journal*. Wall Street Journal, 22 Apr. 2013. Web. 31 May 2013.

6. Alan Cullison, Paul Sonne, and Jennifer Levitz. "Life in America Unraveled for Brothers." *Wall Street Journal*. Wall Street Journal, 20 Apr. 2013. Web. 29 July 2013.

7. Michiko Kakutani. "Unraveling Boston Suspects' Online Lives, Link by Link." *New York Times*. New York Times, 23 Apr. 2013. Web. 31 May 2013.

8. Katharine Q. Seelye and Ian Lovett. "After Attack, Suspects Returned to Routines, Raising No Suspicions." *New York Times*. New York Times, 26 Apr. 2013. Web. 29 July 2013.

9. Erica Goode and Serge F. Kovaleski. "Boy at Home in U.S., Swayed by One Who Wasn't." *New York Times*. New York Times, 19 Apr. 2013. Web. 20 May 2013.

## Chapter 6. Becoming Radical

1. Alan Cullison, Paul Sonne, Anton Troianovski, and David George-Cosh. "Turn to Religion Split Suspects' Home." *Wall Street Journal*. Wall Street Journal, 22 Apr. 2013. Web. 31 May 2013.

2. Suntta Sohrabji. "Boston Marathon Bombing: Are Muslims Always First Suspects, Ponders Community?" *India West*. India West, 26 Apr. 2013. *Newspaper Source Plus*. Web. 25 May 2013.

3. Michael Wines. "The Dark Side, Carefully Masked." *New York Times*. New York Times, 4 May 2013. Web. 30 May 2013.

4. Scott Shane. "A Homemade Style of Terror: Jihadists Push New Tactics." *New York Times*. New York Times, 5 May 2013. Web. 29 July 2013.

5. Ibid.

6. Scott Shane. "Suspects with Foot in 2 Worlds, Perhaps Echoing Plots of Past." *New York Times*. New York Times, 20 Apr. 2013. Web. 30 May 2013.

7. "Boston Marathon Bombings: Suspect Dzhokhar Tsarnaev Left Message in Boat Calling Victims 'Collateral Damage.'" *CBS News*. CBS News, 16 May 2013. Web. 31 May 2013.

## Chapter 7. Seeking Justice

1. "Boston Marathon Bombing Suspect Charged with Using a WMD." *CNN Transcripts*. CNN, 23 Apr. 2010. Web. 29 July 2013.

2. Ashby Jones. "Highlights from Complaint against Boston Bombing Suspect." *Wall Street Journal*. Wall Street Journal, 22 Apr. 2013. Web. 29 July 2013.

3. "Post-ABC Poll: Prosecution of Boston Bombing Suspect." *Washington Post*. Washington Post, 1 May 2013. Web. 29 July 2013.

4. Ashby Jones. "Prosecutors Plot Strategic Course." *Wall Street Journal*. Wall Street Journal, 21 Apr. 2013. Web. 29 July 2013.

## Chapter 8. New Terror Threats and Public Policy

1. Scott Shane. "A Homemade Style of Terror: Jihadists Push New Tactics." *New York Times*. New York Times, 5 May 2013. Web. 29 July 2013.

2. Mark Clayton. "Boston Marathon Bombing: Is American Jihadism on the Rise?" *Christian Science Monitor*. Christian Science Monitor, 23 Apr. 2013. *MasterFILE Premier*. Web. 25 May 2013.

3. Ken Belson. "Security Experts Ponder Whether Any Long Race Can Be Completely Safe." *New York Times*. New York Times, 16 Apr. 2013. Web. 29 July 2013.

4. Alicia A. Caldwell and Eileen Sullivan. "Top Boston Cop OK with More Cameras in City." *Associated Press*. Associated Press, 9 May 2013. *EBSCO News*. Web. 27 May 2013.

5. Mark Landler and Dalia Sussman. "Poll Finds Strong Acceptance for Public Surveillance." *New York Times*. New York Times, 30 Apr. 2013. Web. 29 July 2013.

6. Ken Belson. "Security Experts Ponder Whether Any Long Race Can Be Completely Safe." *New York Times*. New York Times, 16 Apr. 2013. Web. 29 July 2013.

7. Sara Murray, Siobhan Hughes, and Peter Nicholas. "Boston Attacks Complicate Immigration Debate." *New York Times*. New York Times, 19 Apr. 2013. Web. 29 July 2013.

## Chapter 9. Boston Strong

1. Brent Forester. "Boston Marathon Runner & Psychiatrist Shares Personal Story of Patriots' Day 2013." *American Psychiatric Association*. American Psychiatric Association, 29 Apr. 2013. Web. 29 July 2013.

2. Jason Gay. "'Boston Billy' Won't Stop Running." *Wall Street Journal*. Wall Street Journal, 17 Apr. 2013. Web. 29 July 2013.

3. Jonathon Gatehouse and Martin Patriquin. "Boston Bleeds." *Maclean's*. Maclean's, 20 Apr. 2013. Web. 29 July 2013.

4. Scott Smith. "Thousands Run Final Mile of Boston Marathon." *AP English Worldstream*. Associated Press, 25 May 2013. *EBSCO News*. Web. 30 May 2013.

5. Lester Holt. "Prosthetics Advances Made for War Hold Hope for Boston Victims." *NBC News*. NBC News, 28 Apr. 2013. Web. 29 July 2013.

6. Callum Borchers. "Advances in Prosthetics Will Aid Bomb Victims." *Boston Globe*. Boston Globe, 18 Apr. 2013. Web. 29 July 2013.

7. Jennifer Levitz. "Boston Bomb Victims Begin Resuming Lives." *Wall Street Journal*. Wall Street Journal, 10 May 2013. Web. 29 July 2013.

8. Lindsey Tanner. "Boston Victims Face Huge Bills; Donations Pour In." *Associated Press*. Associated Press, 26 Apr. 2013. Web. 29 July 2013.

9. "The One Fund." *The One Fund*. The One Fund, 2013. Web. 29 July 2013.

10. Doug Most. "One Fund Concert Lacked Benefit of TV." *Boston Globe*. Boston Globe, May 2013. Web. 29 July 2013.

11. "Boston Marathon Gives Runners Second Chance to Finish." *USA Today*. USA Today, 16 May 2013. Web. 29 July 2013.

12. Michael Martinez. "Boston Amputee Victims Urged to 'Slay the Monster' with Recovery." *CNN*. CNN, 24 Apr. 2013. Web. 29 July 2013.

13. Brad Knickerbocker. "Did Boston Marathon Bombing Suspects' Mother Push Them Toward Jihad?" *Christian Science Monitor*. Christian Science Monitor, 28 Apr. 2013. *MasterFILE Premier*. Web. 28 May 2013.

14. Michael R. Gordon. "Boston Marathon Winner Will Donate His Medal." *New York Times*. New York Times, 26 May 2013. Web. 29 July 2013.

# INDEX

## ABOUT THE AUTHOR

Valerie Bodden is a freelance author and editor. She has written more than 100 nonfiction children's books. Her books have received positive reviews from *School Library Journal*, *Booklist*, *Children's Literature*, *ForeWord Magazine*, *Horn Book Guide*, *VOYA*, and *Library Media Connection*. Bodden lives in Wisconsin with her husband and four children.

## ABOUT THE CONSULTANT

Morris A. Taylor is an associate professor in the Department of Public Administration & Policy Analysis at Southern Illinois University in Edwardsville Illinois (SIUE). At SIUE since 1997, he has taught graduate courses in public management, policy analysis, public law, program evaluation, ethics, homeland security, and public safety administration. He also serves as an adjunct professor at Northwestern University in Chicago where he teaches the graduate course Fundamentals of Public Administration in their Master of Public Policy & Administration program. Prior to his academic career, Dr. Taylor was an administrator with the Social Security Administration in Saint Louis, Missouri. He has also served as a Saint Louis City and Saint Louis County police officer during the 1970s; and from 2004–2005 he served as the Ira Glasser Racial Justice Fellow for the American Civil Liberties Union of Eastern Missouri. While working with the ACLU he investigated and conducted research on racial profiling and police misconduct. Taylor received his PhD in Public Policy Analysis with a specialization in social jurisprudence from Saint Louis University in Saint Louis, Missouri.